FORGETTING THOSE THINGS WHICH ARE BEHIND

Free to Move Forward

BETHANY BOWMAN

DEDICATION

Thank you, Jesus, for placing this book on the inside of me. I no longer have to remember the past; I can move forward and forget that which is behind. I love you, Jesus!

Thank you to my husband, my biggest supporter. You have been there even when my past was my present you were with me. I love you.

To all of our children, I love you all so much. All of you have supported me in some way. Thank you!

To my apostle and pastors, thank you! To my family and friends, thank you! To all the supporters out there. Thank you!

∽

TABLE OF CONTENTS

Foreword   vii
Introduction   ix
Prayer   xi

1. There Is A Story   1
Prayer   3
2. Forgive   5
Prayer   7
3. Living Again   9
Prayer   11
4. Don't Repeat The Past   13
Prayer   15
5. The Mind Of Christ   17
Prayer   19
6. Get Rid Of Suppressed Pain   21
Prayer   23
7. Walk By Faith   25
Prayer   28
8. Be Done With Condemnation   29
Prayer   32
9. What Are You Thinking About?   33
Prayer   35
10. In Pursuit Of Jesus   37
Prayer   39
11. Forget To Move Forward   41

Prayer   45
Conclusion   47
Testimony   49
Prayer   51
Call To Salvation   53
Spiritual Reflection   57

FOREWORD

One of the primary reasons people are unable to attain or accomplish anything is their failure to press. Yes, there is pain in the press. There is peril in the press. However, with the press comes a promise! If you are going to attain, you must press! If you are going to press, you must let go of the pain of the past.

Forgetting has everything to do with breaking free from the debilitating memory of the past. To *forget* is ultimately to *release*. Whatever *it* is for you, know that it's in reach, but you will not fulfill your destiny until you release the past.

Bethany Bowman is the perfect portrait of what the Philippians 3:13-14 writer declares: "Brethren, I count not myself to have apprehended: but this one thing I do, forgetting those things which are behind, and reaching forth unto those things which are before, I press toward the mark for the prize of the high calling of God in Christ Jesus." Heaven is the prize of the high calling! The prize we fight for and run for and wrestle for. It must be our aim in all that we do.

For years, I have watched God consistently and deliberately display His faithfulness and grace within Bethany's life. Bethany is acquainted with pain, peril, pressing, and promise. This book will help you discover the courage and confidence required to heal, forgive, forget, release and fulfill your destiny! We're all after promise on earth and in eternity. We're all after destiny. We're all after the mark of the high calling: heaven. *Forgetting Those Things Which Are Behind* is the perfect field guide, recipe, and bridge to breakthrough!

MARCUS A. TAYLOR
Lead Pastor of Resurrection Church
Cleveland, OH

~

INTRODUCTION

Oftentimes in life, we face many different obstacles, and some we think are easier to get over than others, but the truth is, we can forget. I've heard most people say that someone has selective hearing. Well, we can apply that to that we choose to forget. We can really select our memories at times. The things that we did we forget but the things that others have done we are so good at remembering and replaying. This book is all about forgetting. The time has passed for us to remember certain things.

God has bigger and better for us in the future, but we must decide to forget the past. We can't bring the old into the new. If you do, you will literally stunt your spiritual growth. As you read this book, let everything drop off that shouldn't be and pick up that which God desires for your life. I pray that you are truly Blessed.

~

"Brethren, I count not myself to have apprehended: but this one thing I do, forgetting those things which are behind, and reaching forth unto those things which are before, I press toward the mark for the prize of the high calling of God in Christ Jesus."

— *PHILIPPIANS 3:13-14*

PRAYER

Lord, I thank you for the opportunity to speak to your people. I am nothing without you. You are God almighty. We can overcome anything through you. You are our beginning and end. Touch every heart, Lord Jesus, that reads this book. Transform every mind and burn up that which is wicked in the imaginations of your people. Give your people the strength to forget that which is behind that they may obtain that which is ahead. Allow forgiveness to manifest in every home, job, and church. You be exalted, Lord Jesus. Thank you for your love. I believe eyes will come open and purpose will be birthed. In Jesus' name, I pray. Amen!

～

Chapter One

THERE IS A STORY

We all have a story, in fact, I spoke a little about mine in my first book, *I Was Anointed For This*. In that book, it was time for me to release my story so that God would get the glory. It was where I was and now a place that others may be in, so for that reason, I will leave it on the shelves though I am in a new chapter.

Jesus wants glory in all that we have come through. If it's not for his glory that we remember or even share, it's best we forget. Sometimes the very memory can be toxic that you hold on to, and it will destroy you. You can not truly move forward if you live in the past. Everyone on this earth has been a victim or an offender.

We all may have a story, but it should not be exalted above our Savior. However, this is what we do when we feel victimized. We make the story bigger than the glory, and so we get stuck. You may even feel condemned. The enemy would love for you to live in pity instead of praise. Praise God for what you have overcome.

You may have been rejected, misunderstood, and abused, but God still deserves our praise. Philippians 3:13 says, *"Brethren, I count not myself to have apprehended: but this one thing I do, forgetting those things which are behind, and reaching forth unto those things which are before."*

In order to move forward, you must forget that which is behind you. Jesus cares so much for us, but memories of the past can come with bitterness. Even if someone has wronged you, you are no better than the wrong that was done to you when you choose to live in that pain. I only want to be reminded when God uses it to bring someone out. Look back to say, "Thank you, Jesus," but never to complain or be bitter.

None of us has received the punishment for which we deserve. Why? Because of God's mercy. So you may have a story, but you are not alone. Jesus also has a story, a story that brought freedom and salvation to us. At any point, Jesus could have complained and refused to die, but He said, "Forgive them, Father, for they know not what they do." Jesus knew what was ahead. He laid down his life regardless of his story. We must press on. Heaven awaits us. Romans 8:35-39 says, *"Who shall separate us from the love of Christ? Shall tribulation, or distress, or persecution, or famine, or nakedness, or peril, or sword? As it is written, For thy sake we are killed all the day long; we are accounted as sheep for the slaughter. Nay, in all these things we are more than conquerors through him that loved us. For I am persuaded, that neither death, nor life, nor angels, nor principalities, nor powers, nor things present, nor things to come, nor height, nor depth, nor any other creature, shall be able to separate us from the love of God, which is in Christ Jesus our Lord."*

PRAYER

Lord Jesus, my prayer for your people is that they forget their story and remember yours. Help them remember how you died and rose just for us. Don't allow them to stay stuck in the past but help them to know that you have so much more for them. I pray that they are no longer hindered because of their memory. I pray that you heal them, Lord, from the inside out.

Get glory out of everything they have been through and teach them how to lean and depend on you. I cast down every image and feeling that would cause them to hold on to anything behind them. Lead them and guide them for your purpose and your plan only. In Jesus' name! Amen!

Chapter Two

FORGIVE

"Then Peter opened his mouth, and said, of a truth I perceive that God is no respecter of persons."

— ACTS 10:34

---

*W*hy do I start with this scripture? I start with this scripture because sometimes we go through things in our lives that make us feel justified, but we are not. God will not overlook our wrong because wrong was done to us. He has no favorites. Just as we love our children the same, He also loves us the same.

Forgiveness can not happen when you choose not to forget. I know. It sounds crazy, right? How can I forget when I am human and am continuously reminded? Forgetting is a choice. It is not something that we suppress, but it is the choice to say, "I was wronged, but I have also wronged."

We can not dwell on the past. We can't change it anyway. What we can do is learn from it and refuse to hold someone in bondage. Let's be honest. We don't wish to be held there. I asked the Lord to remove that which would cause me to be bitter, and I don't replay it. You have to lay it down and move on.

Romans 8:28 says, *"And we know that all things work together for good to them that love God, to them who are the called according to his purpose."* There is nothing that you have gone through that took God by surprise. Allow your past to push you to promise. If we do not forgive, we won't be forgiven.

Matthew 6:14-15 states, *"For if ye forgive men their trespasses, your heavenly Father will also forgive you: But if ye forgive not men their trespasses, neither will your Father forgive your trespasses."* We tend to want to forget the wrong we have done but hold to that which was done to us. However, God does not want that from us. God wants us to forgive and forget. You may not realize that you enter into a new year with the same mindset when you don't forget, which keeps you from fulfilling your destiny. Things may be attached to you because of your unwillingness to forget. Jesus could have come back in moments when we refuse to forget, and hell could have easily been our destination, but he forgave our sins. God's forgiveness is continuous.

Romans 6:1-2 says, *"What shall we say then? Shall we continue in sin, that grace may abound? God forbid. How shall we, that are dead to sin, live any longer therein?"* Just because we have a forgiving God, we cannot live as if grace will always be there. If you can not find the strength to forgive and forget, it's because this strength is not in you and you need Jesus. 2 Corinthians 12:10 states, *"Therefore I take pleasure in infirmities, in reproaches, in necessities, in persecutions, in distresses for Christ's sake: for when I am weak, then am I strong."* Your strength is found in the Lord. Nehemiah 8:10 says, *"Then he said unto them, Go your way, eat the fat, and drink the sweet, and send portions unto them for whom nothing is prepared: for this day is holy unto our Lord: neither be ye sorry; for the joy of the LORD is your strength."* Through the strength of the Lord, it is possible to forgive and forget.

PRAYER

Thank you, Jesus, that you are able and willing to forgive our sins. I pray that your people would show mercy just as you have shown it to them. I rebuke all unforgiveness and bitterness. I plead the Blood of Jesus. I rebuke every spirit that has attempted to keep them from walking in forgiveness. I pray that freedom will be their portion right now in the name of Jesus. All bondage be destroyed in the name of Jesus.

Teach your people just how to forgive. Give them the strength that they need to do so. Heal their broken hearts and help them to walk in forgiveness. Remove every memory that haunts them. Show them how possible it is with you. Thank you, Jesus. It is in your name that we pray! Amen!

~

Chapter Three

LIVING AGAIN

*I*t's time to live again. Jesus is life, and in him is no darkness. We can't truly abide in him and he in us if we have the past corrupting our very thoughts. If you want to live again or live at all, you must release your past. Isaiah 43:18-19 says, *"Remember ye not the former things, neither consider the things of old. Behold, I will do a new thing; now it shall spring forth; shall ye not know it? I will even make a way in the wilderness, and rivers in the desert."* The Lord wants to do a new thing in you and me. He will not do new in old. His Word commands us to forget the former things. If he commands it, it can be done.

God is a good father. Something great awaits you if you would just leave the past behind. I never knew what it was to live until I began to walk in forgiveness, compassion, and love. I truly know how to move forward, and I don't just know, but I am doing it.

We get so caught up in being a victim that we don't realize that we can be offending ourselves. The past has no place with me unless I am praising because I am free from it. I look back to say, "Thank God."

My past keeps me humble. I can see people and not think that they are too dirty because my past was also dirty. The past wants to condemn you. If you dwell on it for the wrong reasons, it can cause you to go back from what you have been freed from.

I think about Paul and how he had to be blinded by the Lord to see. When he was converted and began to preach the Gospel, though he had once persecuted people because of it, those people weren't willing to forget. Some wanted to bring up his past, but you can't live in the past or care about those around that have an opinion about your past.

John 8:36 states, *"If the Son therefore shall make you free, ye shall be free indeed."* If the Lord had brought up those individuals' past, they wouldn't have even been focused on Paul's past. When the Lord sets us free, we are free. We don't have to walk in condemnation. You are free to live.

Romans 8:1-2 states, *"There is therefore now no condemnation to them which are in Christ Jesus, who walk not after the flesh, but after the Spirit. For the law of the Spirit of life in Christ Jesus hath made me free from the law of sin and death."* Forsake the lies of satan that come to convince you that you are not forgiven. God has such a plan for our future. The past has nothing on the future that is before us.

Romans 8:18 says, *"For I reckon that the sufferings of this present time are not worthy to be compared with the glory which shall be revealed in us."* Some have good memories of the past, and some have terrible memories, but regardless of what's behind, you must move forward. Make new memories, walk in the newness of life that Christ has for you.

It's so sad that so many people die in their past and don't even realize it. Some people were once young and now are old, and they are still hurting from betrayal or loss. This is what Paul says in his memory. Psalms 37:25 says, *"I have been young, and now am old; yet have I not seen the righteous forsaken, nor his seed begging bread."* This brings Glory to God. He remembers that he has never been forsaken nor seen it. Remember what God has done for you if you should remember anything.

PRAYER

Thank you, Jesus, that you are life. Help your people to choose to live again through you. Lift up their heads. Show them that there is no life in darkness. Give them hope again. I pray that they leave the past in the past. Breathe upon them so that they may feel your Love and stand on your strength. Restore what was lost. Make them know that you are with them.

Help your people to make a decision today that they will live and not die. Help them stand even when they feel weak. Remove their feet from the edge and cover them with blood. I thank you right now that it is so, in Jesus' name! Amen!

∾

Chapter Four

DON'T REPEAT THE PAST

*D*id you know that most people avoid family gatherings because of the constant replay of the past? You may be causing someone memories that they do not wish to relive. For example, if I am now saved, I would not like to hear how angry I used to be. Some things are better left in the past. Gather with people you love and begin again from a new place with new memories.

God does something new in us each and every day. If He forgets things, why can't we? What you may think is funny may result in someone feeling pain again. We should not be a stumbling block for someone. How embarrassing would it be for you, for the first time, to bring home your family to meet other families, and what was presented were things the Lord forgave? I believe it would really hurt and may even cause someone to be angry, which is the door to sin. Ephesians 4:26 says, *"Be ye angry, and sin not: let not the sun go down upon your wrath."*

We need not provoke one another, and sometimes, this is what we do without even being aware of it. We need to forget our past and the past of others. Romans 12:2 says, *"And be not conformed to this world: but be ye transformed by the renewing of your mind, that ye may prove what is that good, and acceptable, and perfect, will of God."*

Did you know that if your mind is transformed, you will not even dwell on the things of old? Refuse to conform, especially if the past is dark. Philippians 4:8 states, *"Finally, brethren, whatsoever things are true, whatsoever things are honest, whatsoever things are just, whatsoever things are pure, whatsoever things are lovely, whatsoever things are of good report; if there be any virtue, and if there be any praise, think on these things."*

What is good and acceptable to the Lord that you can think on? Also, ask God for a clean heart because my thoughts will follow if my heart is right.

Psalm 51:10 says, *"Create in me a clean heart, O God; and renew a right spirit within me."* Change and chains don't match. You have to allow God to empty you and change your very conversations because the past conversations will hold you in chains. Break free in the name of Jesus! You can walk away cold turkey!

Many people can't break addiction because they remember when. I'm telling you not to look back. You must be purified, completely washed clean, and surrender to Jesus. Once you are set free, you don't need to look back unless you are thanking God that he brought you out. Some people can not handle the look back, and it might cause you to be entangled again. Many have relapsed from looking back, but I tell you to look forward. There is much more ahead than what is behind. Galatians 5:1 states, *"Stand fast therefore in the liberty wherewith Christ hath made us free, and be not entangled again with the yoke of bondage."*

PRAYER

Lord, I pray right now in the name of Jesus that families will be restored and that your wisdom will be given to the reader, and they will know when to speak and when to be silent. I come against the memories of addictions, the feeling that comes with the memory. Clean up every heart, Lord, where they will desire to birth that which is good and forget that which is behind. In Jesus' name, I pray. Amen!

~

Chapter Five

THE MIND OF CHRIST

"Let this mind be in you, which was also in Christ Jesus:"

— *PHILIPPIANS 2:5*

---

*W*hat we need is the mind of Christ. Isaiah 55:8-9 states, *"For my thoughts are not your thoughts, neither are your ways my ways, saith the Lord. For as the heavens are higher than the earth, so are my ways higher than your ways, and my thoughts than your thoughts."*

The mind of Christ thinks nowhere near the frequency of our minds. We need His mind to be in us, for it is not corrupt and holds no wickedness. The mind of Christ has no negativity in it. Though we have good memories behind us, our mind reflects the bad most of the time. This is not pleasing unto the Lord. What will reflect His glory? Doing and thinking on all of those things that please Him. Pray for the mind of Christ to dwell in you. You can control your thoughts. 2 Corinthians 10:5 says, *"Casting down imaginations, and every high thing that exalteth itself against the knowledge of God, and bringing into captivity every thought to the obedience of*

Christ;" The moment the past comes to your mind, you can cast it down before it comes out of your mouth.

John 8:36 states, *"If the Son therefore shall make you free, ye shall be free indeed."* The weapon I use to fight with was once a weapon that was used against me. The enemy wants you to relive your past because he knows that there is no use in the past. You should be approaching the future. Satan is very crafty, and you must know what weapons he will use against you and destroy them.

Your mind can be a place that God dwells or a playing field for the enemy. Satan studies that which would make us tick. He sends assignments through those doors of the past that you forgot to completely shut.

You must go back and shut the door so that you can forget. If I was preparing to fight someone, I am watching for the weakness of my weapon versus theirs, and because I'm going to win, it may not even be a fair fight. Satan fights dirty because he is. He will even set you up to destroy yourself. This is his job.

John 10:10 says, *"The thief cometh not, but for to steal, and to kill, and to destroy: I am come that they might have life, and that they might have it more abundantly."*

However, the Lord desires to give us life. He is that life. Therefore we must hunger after him to have the mind of Christ. Matthew 5:6 states, *Blessed are they which do hunger and thirst after righteousness: for they shall be filled.*

PRAYER

Lord Jesus, help your people to operate as you would have them, forsaking all ungodly thinking and taking on the mind of Christ, forgetting who they once were or how they once perceived their lives. Transform their minds. Renew them today, Lord. Search their hearts. Give them your love and your peace. Place freedom in their thoughts and cause all ill thinking to be destroyed in the name of Jesus. I believe that you are moving in this moment, and I thank you in Jesus' name! Amen!

❧

Chapter Six

GET RID OF SUPPRESSED PAIN

Some things that you may have been through may have been so painful that you buried them. We often think that we have given it to God, but you just forgot about it. Sometimes you have to remember in order to forget. I know what you're thinking. What does she mean? Well, bitterness and unforgiveness have been known to lie dormant. We have to ask God to search us, and when He does search us, He will expose what is in us. Psalm 139 23-24 says, *"Search me, O God, and know my heart: try me, and know my thoughts: And see if there be any wicked way in me, and lead me in the way everlasting."*

The Bible tells us that if something is wrong with us, it will be revealed to us. *Philippians 3:15 says, "Let us, therefore, as many as be perfect, be thus minded: and if in any thing ye be otherwise minded, God shall reveal even this unto you."* The remembrance of what is in you is not for the purpose of reliving but relieving. You must release all that's not like God. Renounce all wickedness that is suppressed deep in your heart.

Proverbs 4:23 states, *"Keep thy heart with all diligence; for out of it are the issues of life."* That which is in you will be thought out and brought out. You must be free, in Jesus' name. I remember a time in my life that I wore a smile on my face that was so bright people began to call me sunshine, and some called me smiley. I had gone through some things, but my smile was a reflection of the condition of my heart. There was also a period where things that were suppressed began to come forth, and it was evident on my face. I didn't yet know why my face looked sad to other people; I thought I was perfectly fine.

I began a new church years ago that is now my church home, a place of love where I was constantly told to smile. It irritated me because I thought that I was smiling. One day I asked God about my face because I felt so misunderstood. He showed me it was the condition of my heart.

We truly act out what is on the inside of us, even if you don't even know it. The number one excuse that I have both heard and said is, "this is how I am," but it's not true. God is love! If we love God, we will walk in that love and reflect that love. John 14:15 says, *"If ye love me, keep my commandments."*

I had to abandon what I thought I should look like because it did not look like my Father, and when you truly get to the root of a thing, you will then produce good fruit. We can't get good fruit from a rotten tree, so if dead things are lying dormant in you, ask God to purge you. Everything that was suppressed will be burned up with Holy Fire. Hebrews 12:29 says, *"For our God is a consuming fire."*

PRAYER

Lord Jesus, thank you that you see all and you know all. Thank you that nothing has and never will take you by surprise. I lift up every reader at this moment, and as they pray, I ask you to consume everything that is not like you. Lord Jesus, go deep into their souls and cause them to offer all wickedness to you, all shame God, all bitterness, all things that were buried but not forgiven. Uproot them, Jesus.

Jesus, change the posture of their heart right now. God, you alone are worthy. There is none above you nor beside you. Nothing can stand toe to toe with you. God, at your name, the earth bows. Thank you, Lord, that you are healing right now. Thank you, God, that you do not fail; so God, I thank you and believe it is so. In Jesus' name. Amen.

~

Chapter Seven

WALK BY FAITH

F orgetting takes faith. You must believe that you can forget in order for your thoughts to line up. I have heard some say, "I can forgive, but I can't forget." The devil is a liar. You can forgive and forget. If it weren't so, God wouldn't have told us. When we go to bed at night, we plan out our lives for the next day; that's displaying faith. Well, that same faith has to cause you to forget.

We must trust God to know that if he heals you, he will erase the things that hurt you. Hebrews 11:6, *"But without faith, it is impossible to please him: for he that cometh to God must believe that he is and that he is a rewarder of them that diligently seek him."* We need faith for everything in life. However, we don't always feel that we need faith when we have access to something.

2 Corinthians 5:7 states, *"For we walk by faith, not by sight:"* Faith can't be about what you see but rather what you don't see. Even if there are memories that you want to be gone that are still present at the moment, believe that God will remove those things if they serve him no purpose. We are saved by faith. So if you can believe that, believe that your mind can be healed and have patience for God's timing.

John 10:10 10 says, *"The thief cometh not, but for to steal, and to kill, and to destroy: I am come that they might have life and that they might have it more abundantly."* If the enemy can steal your faith, he has you. Jesus went about and healed many, and by their faith, they were made whole. As God has removed the things on the inside that lied dormant, you now must believe that it is done in Jesus' name. He won't leave you halfway healed as he removes; everything will come into alignment.

Deuteronomy 31:6 states, *"Be strong and of a good courage, fear not, nor be afraid of them: for the Lord thy God, he it is that doth go with thee; he will not fail thee, nor forsake thee."* Hebrews 10:38-39 says, *"Now the just shall live by faith: but if any man draw back, my soul shall have no pleasure in him. But we are not of them who draw back unto perdition, but of them, that believe to the saving of the soul."* Hebrews 11:1 says, *"Now faith is the substance of things hoped for, the evidence of things not seen."*

When I look back over my life, I literally can't remember a time that God has failed me. I expect God to keep me. I expect God to keep my family. I can't see myself without God. I believe in what He said. We can't just quote scriptures; we must also believe them. As I have gotten closer to God, I see things so clear. God has already created our ending, so if he said there is a plan for me, I believe it.

At times things seem totally opposite of what He said. For instance, He may call me healed, and I may feel physical pain now, but because He said it, I keep speaking it until it manifests. Don't hold up your future. Choose to believe. God is faithful. It's not the Lord's desire for you to be tormented in your mind by things you believe He can handle. I serve a big God, and He can surely erase and add. Sometimes Jesus has removed things you try so hard to remember.

I consider myself to have a really good memory, but there are some things that I know existed that I have no recollection of now, and I had to believe it was God. We can't forget on our own. You can only bury it. What's buried comes back, but what has been erased will not return. Even the things that triggered the thoughts will be gone.

Let go of doubt and fear today so that Christ can make you knew. Isaiah 54:17 states, *"No weapon that is formed against thee shall prosper, and every tongue that shall rise against thee in judgment thou shalt condemn. This is the heritage of the servants of the Lord, and their right-eousness is of me, saith the Lord."* Proverbs 3:5-6 says, *"Trust in the Lord with all thine heart; and lean not unto thine own understanding. In all thy ways acknowledge him, and he shall direct thy paths."*

PRAYER

Lord Jesus, you are so amazing. You hold all power in your hands. If you don't do it, it will not be done. Pour faith into your people so that they may believe in the impossible. Thank you for allowing us to believe in you. Thank you that we are not waiting on a God that doesn't move. Since we get to believe, let us not take this opportunity for granted, God. I pray in the name of Jesus that all doubt be silenced, and your people would walk by faith and not by sight.

Show them that you are mighty; show them that you are strong. Thank you, Lord. You are Holy. You are a just God, and the just shall live by faith. I come against false faith in the name of Jesus! Show them their faith. Subtract and add to them, Lord. Where there is lack, restore God. I thank you, in Jesus' name! Amen!

Chapter Eight

BE DONE WITH CONDEMNATION

*T*oday you forgive yourself. The most common thing to remember is our mistakes. Sometimes we can quickly forgive and forget others' mistakes, but we carry our mistakes in our minds. God does not want that for you or me, and today you have to decide that you want to forgive yourself. Romans 8:1 states, *"There is therefore now no condemnation to them which are in Christ Jesus, who walk not after the flesh, but after the Spirit."*

Condemnation is a silent killer. Usually, you tell no one, but you can't help but replay the events in your mind. There is no freedom in that. Satan wants you to stay in that bondage of your past. If it happened yesterday, that's ok. If you repented, it's in your past. Cycles continue when you choose not to let go, and most times, you end up doing something worst because you feel you weren't forgiven the first time. I have seen someone literally become sick and die by replaying the past. There may be death behind you, but there is life in front of you.

Do you know how much Jesus loves you? I am here to tell you He loves you so much that He would instruct you to forget! Unforgiveness is unforgiveness. You have to forgive yourself. There are so many things in the Bible that you can choose to remember that will give you hope. Your past is nothing compared to your future.

Talk to Jesus about your concerns. I promise you He will heal you. Everyone has sinned and done things that they are not proud of, but release it. Let it fade away unless it's here to help. It's like going through your phone looking at photos or phone numbers. You may ask yourself, "Why do I still have this? That was so long ago." Let go of the baggage. Hebrews 12:1 says, *"Wherefore seeing we also are compassed about with so great a cloud of witnesses, let us lay aside every weight, and the sin which doth so easily beset us, and let us run with patience the race that is set before us,"*

Don't allow what happened in your past to keep you from seeing Jesus. Break free from every lie of the enemy in the name of Jesus. Nothing that the enemy has told you is the truth. It's all a lie. Satan wants you to slip up and spend eternity in hell. You have to do what it takes to get free. My brother and sister, I beg you to forget. Time is not on our side. We must be ready when Jesus returns. Forget the foolishness; get right and get ready. Jesus wants to give you peace. Accept His peace.

John 14:27 says, *"Peace I leave with you, my peace I give unto you: not as the world giveth, give I unto you. Let not your heart be troubled, neither let it be afraid."* When you feel like you can't make it and the enemy is trying to take your mind, speak the Word. Psalm 118:17 states, *"I shall not die, but live, and declare the works of the Lord."* Jesus spoke the Word when the enemy tried to tempt Him in the wilderness. You see, the enemy tries to come when he thinks that you are weak, but when you realize the strength of God that lies within you, the enemy will flee and will not come back in that manner again.

We know that the enemy's job is to attack, so we expect it, but he won't try that way again. James 4:7 says, *"Submit yourselves therefore to God. Resist the devil, and he will flee from you."* Every time the past wants to come up, cast it down. Don't leave a little room for it because that is giving the enemy access. Ephesians 4:27 states,

"Neither give place to the devil." We must watch what we entertain, or we will become the entertainment. 1 Peter 5:8 says, *"Be sober, be vigilant; because your adversary the devil, as a roaring lion, walketh about, seeking whom he may devour:"*

PRAYER

I lift you up, Lord Jesus, asking you to remove the burden from your people to carry what you have forgiven. Remind them that you died for their sins and that they can forgive themselves. I rebuke the replay of their sin, for your Word declares that whom the Son sets free is free indeed. Remove every chain, Lord.

I pray that their minds be renewed right now in the name of Jesus! I pray that they receive your forgiveness, healing, and peace. I cancel the very whisper of the enemy. Faith rise. Power rise. In the name of Jesus! Condemnation, go, in the name of Jesus, and do not return! Peace be still! In Jesus' name! Amen!

~

Chapter Nine

WHAT ARE YOU THINKING ABOUT?

*H*ave you ever asked this question to someone that seemed to be present in the body, but you knew that their mind was not? Well, I ask you, what are you thinking about? We have all mastered being present without actually being present. Our mind is always somewhere else, whether it is the morning traffic or the past. There are things in our day that we may have missed because of the past tense. It's time to look past our past. Quickly let things go. The season for living in the past is over.

I promise you don't want to get stuck there. There is joy on the other side. Some may feel that you have been here or there too long, but it's time to get up. I'm reminded of a place that I was in in my past, and God sent a word that told me it was time to get up. That word couldn't have come at a better time. If I had been disobedient, I wouldn't have gotten out. To God be the glory for jolting me out of the past. Once you are healed, it's no reason for you to look back. It will only make you salty like Lot's wife. Genesis 19:26 reminds us, *"But his wife looked back from behind him, and she became a pillar of salt."*

You have been salty enough. The past can't do anything for me unless it's blessing my Jesus. Jesus thought enough about me to bring me out, and if He says, that's enough of the past, that is enough. I don't need a confirmation; that is enough. I want to know what you are doing right now, Jesus. What is my new testimony? What are the great things that are ahead? I'm believing for big things, curses broken, relationships restored. We have no time to be bitter. I ain't dying like that. Forget the thought of who forgot you. Think about the fact that Jesus remembered you. Your story may have been something, but the glory from your story is even better.

Philippians 4:8 says, *"Finally, brethren, whatsoever things are true, whatsoever things are honest, whatsoever things are just, whatsoever things are pure, whatsoever things are lovely, whatsoever things are of good report; if there be any virtue, and if there be any praise, think on these things."*

I've got something to praise about hallelujah! I used to watch the old mothers praise and didn't know why they were praising, so I mocked them to see if I could feel what they were feeling. But now that I know why they were praising, it makes me praise even more. The past is behind, and I'm here to praise about it. That should be enough to make you praise. Whatever you have faced, you are here to praise about it. Hallelujah! Think about the goodness of Jesus, and you will forget your past.

PRAYER

Lord Jesus, cause the thoughts of your people to give you the glory that you are due. Silence the voice of the enemy, Jesus. Let your voice be so loud. Let the praises of your people be so big. I tear down every image that the enemy has presented before them. Burn up the bondage in their mind, God. Let your people arise in power, rebuking every lie, standing on your Word, Lord Jesus. Give them focus, give them their bounce back. I rebuke pride, deceit, and complaint in the name of Jesus. Release your fire now, God. Release! Hallelujah in the name of Jesus. Let them become thirsty for you so much that they can't even remember what hurt them before you healed them. It is in the name of Jesus that I pray. Amen!

Chapter Ten

IN PURSUIT OF JESUS

"Blessed are they which do hunger and thirst after righteousness: for they shall be filled."

— MATTHEW 5:6

*T*here is no time to remember when you truly are about your Father's business. John 14:15 states, *"If ye love me, keep my commandments."* Since memories often bring up painful events, we need to love God enough to say, "No matter what my past looks like, I love you." Forsake your feelings about the matter, be pleasing to the Lord at all cost.

When you have a made-up mind to serve the Lord, there is no looking back. Luke 9:62 states, *"And Jesus said unto him, No man, having put his hand to the plough, and looking back, is fit for the kingdom of God."* There is no wavering in Christ. Make up your mind to be healed. James 1:8 states, *"A double minded man is unstable in all his ways."* My Apostle always says it all points back to how much you love Jesus. I agree with what he said because we have to pursue

Jesus without compromise. Our love for Christ is not to just be spoken but acted out.

We have to pursue Jesus relentlessly. If He had chosen to remember how we crucified Him, our future would not be waiting on us. Everybody likes to speak about Judas, but if we are not pursuing righteousness, then we too become a "Judas" because we cannot serve to masters. Judas chose to pursue his lust for money, and it's possible that your past could be the very reason that you betray Jesus. There is brokenness, bitterness, and addictions in the past, so leave them there. Anything that's not for God is against Him.

Matthew 6:33 says, *"But seek ye first the kingdom of God, and his righteousness; and all these things shall be added unto you."* As you pursue the Lord first, your pain, shame, and regrets will be removed; peace, joy, and love will be added. This is the Word of God, and it does not lie. He will add as you seek Him.

Understand that the pursuit of Jesus uncovers things, but there is healing in the uncovering. Never be afraid to seek Jesus. He cares so much for you and me. Nothing in our past would cause Him to look at us strange or avoid us. Jesus is the one person that you can pursue and pour out on.

Remember to run with patience, but run! Run far from your past, run to all that Jesus is. You will have for sure safety in Jesus. He desires to make you new. Revelation 21:5 says, *"And he that sat upon the throne said, Behold, I make all things new. And he said unto me, Write: for these words are true and faithful."* Will you allow Jesus to make you new today? Forget that which is behind and prepare for what is ahead.

PRAYER

Lord, thank you for being available to us. Thank you for not hiding and welcoming us with open arms. I'm praying right now that your people will begin to get hungry for you, turning away from all wickedness. Place in them the desire to please you. Touch their minds when they go to sleep and when they wake up. Strip them of all things that will cause them to crave anything other than you.

Pour out your peace. Give them beauty for ashes. Thank you for being a good Father. We need you, Jesus. The world can't give us life. I pray that your people release all fear that will keep them from pursuing you. Uproot every stronghold that has kept them from becoming who you have called them to be. I bind up all idols and images that have defiled the thoughts of your people. I am praying for freedom right now and that as you remove, you replace. I pray these things in Jesus' name. Amen!

∽

Chapter Eleven

FORGET TO MOVE FORWARD

*F*orget in order to move forward, but don't forget to move forward. I am going to now break down two different stories in the Bible that discuss moving forward - the man at the Pool of Bethesda and the woman with the issue of blood. Let us first began with John 5:1-14, which tells the story of the man at the pool of Bethesda:

> *After this there was a feast of the Jews; and Jesus went up to*
> *Jerusalem. Now there is at Jerusalem by the sheep market a pool,*
> *which is called in the Hebrew tongue Bethesda, having five porches.*
> *In these lay a great multitude of impotent folk, of blind, halt, with-*
> *ered, waiting for the moving of the water. For an angel went down*
> *at a certain season into the pool, and troubled the water: whosoever*
> *then first after the troubling of the water stepped in was made whole*
> *of whatsoever disease he had. And a certain man was there, which*
> *had an infirmity thirty and eight years.*
>
> *When Jesus saw him lie, and knew that he had been now a long time*
> *in that case, he saith unto him, Wilt thou be made whole? The impo-*
> *tent man answered him, Sir, I have no man, when the water is trou-*
> *bled, to put me into the pool: but while I am coming, another*

steppeth down before me. Jesus saith unto him, Rise, take up thy
bed, and walk. And immediately the man was made whole, and took
up his bed, and walked: and on the same day was the sabbath.

The Jews therefore said unto him that was cured, It is the sabbath
day: it is not lawful for thee to carry thy bed. He answered them, He
that made me whole, the same said unto me, Take up thy bed, and
walk. Then asked they him, What man is that which said unto thee,
Take up thy bed, and walk? And he that was healed wist not who it
was: for Jesus had conveyed himself away, a multitude being in that
place.
Afterward Jesus findeth him in the temple, and said unto him,
Behold, thou art made whole: sin no more, lest a worse thing come
unto thee.

What we have here is a man who is sick and had been sick for a very long time, 38 years to be exact. Healing took place only at certain times. Instead of him fighting to be healed, he decided to lie there and blame the people around him because they did not help him. This had been 38 years, though.

Sometimes we hold on to thoughts when we have the opportunity to forget who wasn't there, who didn't believe, and who abused us. We have chosen to lie their bitter and broken when healing could take place with just one decision and, in his case, a couple of steps.

Jesus asked this man the question, "Wilt thou be made whole?" This was when he began to look back on why he could not be healed, but all Jesus wanted to know was if he wanted to be "whole." In the midst of his excuses, Jesus told him to rise and take his bed up. Don't waste time trying to make excuses in your mind why you can't move forward when Jesus is right in front of you asking, "Wilt thou be made whole?" All you have to do is decide to move forward. One choice could change your life.

Understand also that someone or some thought will always be there. *How did this happen? It's not time.* Don't let your reply be like this man who once was sick. "He that made me whole told me to rise up and walk." When you begin to walk, do not look back and don't sin anymore. Don't open the door to those thoughts that held you. Don't revisit the place where you were hurt. Close the door, shut the window, and run far from that place in Jesus's name! Ephesians 4:27 says, *"Neither give place to the devil."* Now we will look at Luke 8:43-48, where it speaks of the woman with the issue of blood and learn how she walks away from her past.

> *And a woman having an issue of blood twelve years, which had spent all her living upon physicians, neither could be healed of any, Came behind him, and touched the border of his garment: and immediately her issue of blood stanched. And Jesus said, Who touched me? When all denied, Peter and they that were with him said, Master, the multitude throng thee and press thee, and sayest thou, Who touched me? And Jesus said, Somebody hath touched me: for I perceive that virtue is gone out of me. And when the woman saw that she was not hid, she came trembling, and falling down before him, she declared unto him before all the people for what cause she had touched him, and how she was healed immediately. And he said unto her, Daughter, be of good comfort: thy faith hath made thee whole; go in peace.*

Now we have here a woman that had been sick for 12 years. She tried other alternatives, and when those didn't work, she pursued Jesus. She had heard that Jesus was passing by, and this woman got up! This woman could have chosen to stay there in her pain and her stench, but she knew that she would be healed if she just touched Jesus. When you decide to get up, you have no choice but to forget where you once laid. If the memory of where she came from had overtaken her, she probably would have been there another 12 years. This woman did not listen to her pain or pay attention to people starring at her as she began to press through the crowd.

This woman decides to press, and if you want to forget, you must press. Only because of the woman's press was she able to be healed. It took faith for this woman to move forward. She probably was kicked, stepped on, and talked about, but she continued to press. Jesus knew when she touched Him, and he told her that her faith had made her whole.

I'm writing you now to let you know that your faith will make you whole. Don't wait like the man from the Pool of Bethesda. The woman with the issue of blood and the man at the Pool of Bethesda both waited longer than they should have, but she got up and forgot the place she was in and decided to press. Will you decide to press today? Will you allow your faith to make you whole? If we learn anything from the two parables, remember that it was all based on a decision. A decision to blame and remain lame or a decision to get up and chase that great name!

I have been on both sides of these two individuals' decisions and I can tell you that pressing towards Jesus is the best thing you could ever do. It does not pay to hold on to bitterness, but then again, it does. James 1:15 says, *"Then when lust hath conceived, it bringeth forth sin: and sin, when it is finished, bringeth forth death."* It is a good idea to forgive and leave the past in the past. Just as our example of the woman with the issue of blood, she had to leave the place that she laid behind to press. Can you imagine her carrying all of that with her and expecting to be healed?

Jesus even told the man at the pool of Bethesda, "take your bed up" In other words, don't get back in it once you have been healed. Leave no opportunity or room for the old to come into the new. It's far better to forget. Isaiah 43:18-19 says, *"Remember ye not the former things, neither consider the things of old. Behold, I will do a new thing; now it shall spring forth; shall ye not know it? I will even make a way in the wilderness, and rivers in the desert."*

PRAYER

Lord Jesus, I am praying for the readers and asking that you help them get up, in the name of Jesus. I pray that it does not take them another 12 or 38 years to realize that you are a healer. Lord, cause them to carry all of their sicknesses to you. Lord, be their strength. Show them they can not do this on their own but that they need you. Let your name ring in their ears and rest upon their hearts. Remove all issues.

I bind up every curse in the name of Jesus. Heal the memory. Cover the place they once laid so that they can't even see it unless it's for your glory. I plead the Blood of Jesus right now. Shift them and lift them, God. What was meant to kill them, allow it to bless them. Help your people to be free. Let them see the plan of the enemy so that they will not be deceived. I rebuke the fear of getting up. I rebuke the shame that will keep them in that place. Turn their focus to you, Lord.

Remind them that there is a plan and that your Word will not return void. Lord, I thank you now in advance because you are an on-time God, and your healing is permanent. You cannot fail, you will fail, and this we believe! In Jesus' name, I pray. Amen!

∾

CONCLUSION

"There is a way which seemeth right unto a man, but the end thereof are the ways of death."

— *PROVERBS 14:12*

You may feel that it is your God-given right to hold on to that which is behind. I once thought the same; it is our duty to let go and allow God to be God. We can not seek what we are not willing to give. Forgiveness happens as we forgive. The past could be that which motivates you or that which will hold and control you. Therefore we must continue to move forward.

"Trust in the Lord with all thine heart; and lean not unto thine own understanding. In all thy ways acknowledge him, and he shall direct thy paths."

— *PROVERBS 3:5-6*

Move forward even if you don't yet understand. Pray and ask the Lord to lead you, and He will. It may seem scary to leave the past behind because some thoughts literally become a crutch, but once the crutch is gone, you have no choice but to walk by faith and not by sight. Don't allow the past to dictate your future. You can move forward. What you have to remember is that you can't do it on your own. You need Jesus.

"But seek ye first the kingdom of God, and his righteousness; and all these things shall be added unto you."

— *MATTHEW 6:33*

If you never trust anything, trust that God's Word does not lie, and He will take care of you. You can walk away from your past and begin to live as He has created you to, with no images, feelings, or thoughts of the past.

TESTIMONY

Truth be told, I have not always known how to forget that which was behind. I used to think it was ok to live there from time to time, not understanding that the Lord wanted to set me free. The closer I got to Jesus, the more I could see that it was not His will for me to live there and continue to open those doors. I had to learn that I had not forgiven my past; it was lying dormant. How did I know that? I knew because it hurt me to speak about it, and when I did think about it, it was a door to another door that led to bitterness. I love Jesus too much to live in places that he did not design for me, so I knew that it was time to surrender the past to move forward.

You see, the past will destroy your very future if you do not let it go. We can't change our past, but we can change in order for the past not to become the present. Because I have Jesus, I can walk in authority through that name. I do not have to be bound by my mistakes or someone else's.

I chose to be a curse breaker through the Blood of Jesus. The moment I told Satan no, I became a curse breaker. The thoughts that came brought bitterness with them. Just as I rebuked them, you must continue to rebuke the enemy. The enemy is relentless. We have to realize we are in a war. If you don't overcome that which is holding you hostage, it will overcome you. I fight in prayer. Prayer is my connection to the Lord, and it ruins the enemy's plans.

If you really want to be free and move forward, surrender it all to Jesus. I wouldn't be able to write this to you if I hadn't had to do it myself. I am a living testimony. Be encouraged! You can walk in freedom, in Jesus's name! John 8:36 says, *"If the Son therefore shall make you free, ye shall be free indeed."*

PRAYER

Lord Jesus, I come before you, lifting up your people. I am asking you to visit them right where they are. Touch their minds. Reveal to them their hearts. As you reveal their hearts, cause them not to ignore what they see but to give it all to you - every lie, every memory, every corrupt thought. Cause them to surrender.

Open the blind eyes, Lord, so that they may know what hurts you, Jesus. Deliver them from every generational curse Lord and all fear. I rebuke torment and nightmares. Send your consuming fire to burn every idol thought and thing that exalts itself above you. I plead the blood of Jesus. Restore your people. Draw them near you. Cause peace to be their portion. Help them press towards you, Jesus, and forget everything that denies you glory in Jesus's name. Amen.

CALL TO SALVATION

Have you met Jesus yet? I have great news! You can meet him right here in this book. Jesus loves you so much, and if you are ready to move forward, invite him in right now. Say this prayer: Lord Jesus, I am a sinner, and I repent! Come into my heart and transform my mind that I may now live for you and forget that which is behind. Give me all of you, Jesus, and remove those things that hurt you and hinder me. Fill me with your spirit, and use me for your glory from this day forward. In Jesus's name that I pray. Amen!

If you prayed this prayer and you believe, you are saved. However, there is more! According to scripture, we must be baptized in Jesus's name, filled with his spirit, the Holy Ghost, and live holy. We are all being saved, so every day, we must die to ourselves and be obedient to every command that the Word of God gives us. We are one day going to be with Him if we follow His Word. Find a church home where you can be baptized in Jesus's name. It takes more than believing to get us into heaven; we must continue to follow God's plan.

~

"That if thou shalt confess with thy mouth the Lord Jesus, and shalt believe in thine heart that God hath raised him from the dead, thou shalt be saved. For with the heart man believeth unto righteousness; and with the mouth confession is made unto salvation."

    - ROMANS 10: 9-10

"Jesus answered, Verily, verily, I say unto thee, Except a man be born of water and of the Spirit, he cannot enter into the kingdom of God."

    - JOHN 3:5

"Then Peter said unto them, Repent, and be baptized every one of you in the name of Jesus Christ for the remission of sins, and ye shall receive the gift of the Holy Ghost."

    - ACTS 2:38

"And it came to pass, that, while Apollos was at Corinth, Paul having passed through the upper coasts came to Ephesus: and finding certain disciples, He said unto them, Have ye received the Holy Ghost since ye believed? And they said unto him, We have not so much as heard whether there be any Holy Ghost. And he said unto them, Unto what then were ye baptized? And they said, Unto John's baptism. Then said Paul, John verily baptized with the baptism of repentance, saying unto the people, that they should believe on him which should come after him, that is, on Christ Jesus. When they heard this, they were baptized in the name of the Lord Jesus. And when Paul had laid his hands upon them, the Holy Ghost came on them; and they spake with tongues, and prophesied."

    - ACTS 19:2-6

"Thou believest that there is one God; thou doest well: the devils also believe, and tremble."

    - JAMES 2:19

"Blessed are they which do hunger and thirst after righteousness: for they shall be filled."

   - MATTHEW 5:6

"And be not conformed to this world: but be ye transformed by the renewing of your mind, that ye may prove what is that good, and acceptable, and perfect, will of God."

   - ROMANS 12:2

"But as he which hath called you is holy, so be ye holy in all manner of conversation; Because it is written, Be ye holy; for I am holy."

   - 1 PETER 1: 15-16

SPIRITUAL REFLECTION

∾

"Casting down imaginations, and every high thing that exalteth itself against the knowledge of God, and bringing into captivity every thought to the obedience of Christ;"

- 2 CORINTHIANS 10:5

"For we wrestle not against flesh and blood, but against principalities, against powers, against the rulers of the darkness of this world, against spiritual wickedness in high places."

- EPHESIANS 6:12

"Brethren, I count not myself to have apprehended: but this one thing I do, forgetting those things which are behind, and reaching forth unto those things which are before,"

- PHILIPPIANS 3:13

"Remember ye not the former things, neither consider the things of old. Behold, I will do a new thing; now it shall spring forth; shall ye not

know it? I will even make a way in the wilderness, and rivers in the
desert."

   - ISAIAH 43:18

"For we walk by faith, not by sight:"
   - 2 CORINTHIANS 5:7

~

Made in the USA
Middletown, DE
09 May 2021

39289608R00040